RENA SAKELLARIDOU

SEA VOYAGE

RENA SAKELLARIDOU

SEA VOYAGE

PHOTOGRAPHY

ERIETA ATTALI

HATJE
CANTZ

To the memory of my mother.
This journey started on a boat
that, long-forgotten, summer…

PREFACE

This book is about the new headquarters of an internationally renowned Greek maritime group in Athens. In 2012 one of the largest privately owned maritime groups worldwide, Angelicoussis Group, held an invited competition for its new, 30,000-square-meter headquarters, a decision carrying deeper significance amid the country's economic crisis. In the five years before its completion, Agemar was, apart from the new SNFCC cultural center near the waterfront, the only large-scale building to be constructed in Athens.

The proximity to the sea and the maritime nature of the client were coupled with my personal experience: a sea voyage is about a horizon and a direction. The building opens up to the horizon; it reaches for the sea. A Sea Voyage became Agemar's concept.

Agemar is not a corporate building. It is more of a house for a group of companies, a rather big house, though. In my narrative I tell the story of Agemar from the first ideas that shaped it to its final completion; through texts, sketches, drawings, models, and photos produced throughout the building's conception, design implementation, and what I refer to as the "suspended time of construction," I compile a diary on the making of the building. By taking this behind-the-scenes approach, I contemplate the process and, at the same time, I attempt to throw light on how the personal surfaces through the architectural. The voyage to the sea is not only literal; I am interested in the ways our "internal sea" influences what we do and what we are. For I believe that design is the bridging of two worlds: one, our personal world, the "space within," this internal sea of hopes, desires, and all we are; and the other, the external world of reality. Every creative activity integrates the two worlds, or at least tries to. The diary of Agemar is also a personal diary.

In her photographic narrative, on the other hand, Erieta focuses on both Agemar's architecture and its dialogue with the city of Athens. She captures through her lens the various instances of the building, revealing the way Agemar's flowing horizontal lines become literal, and phenomenal reflections of the horizon under the intense Attic light.

The architect and the photographer set up a dialogue between two voices, two points of view.

Athens, July 2019

AGEMAR IS

RENA SAKELLARIDOU

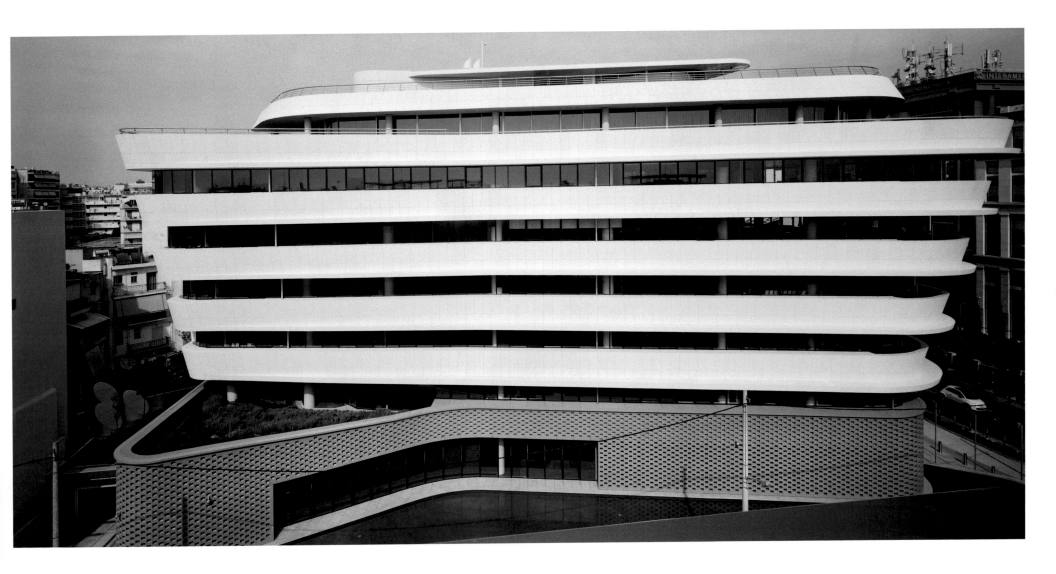

Image courtesy: © Erieta Attali

Athens is

…dense, varied, contradictory.

Even though it has a long waterfront, extending from Piraeus to Faliro and beyond, from the Athens Riviera to the Temple of Apollo in Sounion, the city remains hesitant to its opening to the sea. The sea horizon, on the other hand, relieves the expansiveness of the urban sprawl, while, under the strong Attic light and the bright blue sky, whiteness and shadows become intensified.

Agemar is

…openness to the horizon, fluidity, continuities, whiteness, light-and-shadow composition.

Agemar covers 30,616 square meters of floor area in two buildings. Building A, Administration, houses the entrance foyer, company museum, and library on the ground floor, open-plan offices on five floors, owners' and executive offices on the sixth floor, and an owner's lounge, a canopy, and an extensive garden on the top floor. Building B, Crew, has an amphitheater and a restaurant on the ground floor, offices on three floors, and a roof garden. The two buildings connect underground on four levels, with a company gym and a twenty-five-meter swimming pool, bridge and engine simulators, and auxiliary spaces on the first underground level, and parking for 330 cars on the other three.

Horizontality and directionality are joined together in a fluid geometry that generates the flexible nonfinite form. Both buildings rest on a base covered by a claustra. The base retreats from the street front; its geometry negotiates scale in the urban tissue. Generous "subtractions" bring natural light to the gym/pool and the simulators and mediate the building's relation to the ground. Water surfaces create reflections; nature erodes the base and conquers it.

The long horizontal lines of the "floating in the sea" curved form adapt to the urban scale, create a strong image in the cityscape, and set up a dialogue with the intense Attic light. In a "thick wall" strategy, the fenestration lines transform the view to a "film strip" in the interior. An ellipsoidal atrium creates spatial intelligibility and a play of light and shadow; time and its passing are always present.

As if in a metaphor of a boat at sea, materiality distinguishes between the white of the floating upper part and the gray of the base; white marble cladding, CNC cut with a stainless-steel substructure in the upper part of Building A, a GRC prefabricated claustra and gray sanded marble for the base. Building B, on the other hand, is covered by a vertical garden. Light gray fair-faced concrete elements, anodized aluminum, structural curtain wall systems, "invisible frames" for the executive floor, and flat or curved high-performance glass complete the main material choices. Terraces with local plants create green carpets on different floors, while the top-floor roof garden is shaded by a high-gloss fiberglass/metal canopy with fluid geometry.

Continuities in form and spatial definitions, in material choices and detailing give the interior an airy quality. The void visually connects lobbies on all floors. White-marble curved walls diffuse the limits of space, while semitransparent glass walls hide and reveal views. Public spaces on the ground floor are expansive, both literally and phenomenally; geometry blends with materiality and the reflections of the surrounding water surfaces. A sculptural white-marble wall separates one of the owners' offices from the boardroom and the lobby. By giving them a different atmosphere, spaces such as the company museum, the library, the amphitheater, and the restaurant, and also the gym and the pool, become focal points in the design. The creation of play between reflections and shadows for the museum, warm walnut wood and dark blue for the library, terrazzo and a playful atmosphere for the restaurant, a shiny silver curtain for the amphitheater, soft geometries in terrazzo for the pool area, and mirrors multiplying reflections in the gym contribute to this design choice.

The structure is steel-reinforced concrete. Prestressed beams and metal suspension columns support the large cantilevers. Great care is given to efficient energy consumption and all environmental aspects. Agemar is a LEED Platinum building.

BETWEEN THE CITY AND THE SEA

KAYE GEIPEL

FIVE OBSERVATIONS CONCERNING

RENA SAKELLARIDOU'S AGEMAR HEADQUARTERS

IN THE FALIRO BAY AREA OF ATHENS

Image courtesy: © Erieta Attali

AESTHETICS OF THE HORIZONTAL

On a sunny morning in April 2004, I met with some colleagues from European architecture magazines at Faliro Bay, ready to inspect the newly designed seaside promenade in Athens and the sports facilities for the Olympics. Before things got started, I turned around for a moment to look back at the city. I felt the pull of Syngrou Avenue, the city expressway, which intersects the seaside promenade here like a flow of forces crammed between the densely concentrated urban development of Paleo Faliro and Kallithea before the surging car traffic is then rerouted by the maze of the traffic circle to National Road 91. I was fascinated by this part of Athens, where the rawness of the urban-planning infrastructure and the potentiality of the modern city collide and raise the question of its future development.

The stroll along the seaside at Faliro Bay took place a few weeks before the start of the twenty-eighth Summer Olympic Games in Athens. At the time, I was preparing an issue of *Bauwelt* that only dealt in part with buildings for the Olympics.[1] What interested me above all was the unusual production of the built environment of modern Athens and the *antiparochi* system of the fifties and sixties. I was curious about the buildings that stand out from this small-scale, exemplarily mixed structure. After visiting the buildings for the Olympics, I walked along Syngrou Avenue back to the center of the city and finally stood in front of the remaining part of the Fix brewery by Takis Zenetos and Margaritis Apostolidis, with its façade characterized by vanishing horizontal lines.[2] This central building of Greek postwar modernism, even as an amputated ruin, makes visible the promise of a new relationship between the city, its "grid," and the long-neglected development of the coast—as a stimulus for thinking about the central role of larger urban design components.

The Agemar Headquarters in the Faliro Bay Area

Now that Agemar, the headquarters of the biggest Greek shipping company, has opened fifteen years later in the Kallithea district, this is then not only one of the city's most ambitious construction projects. It is also an urban building block that makes a statement about the relationship between the urban and architectural scales in Athens in an outstanding way.

The architect, Rena Sakellaridou, who besides her architecture office in Athens also teaches design at the university in Thessaloniki, first describes her building with a very personal attribute: "a journey to the sea." To avoid any misunderstandings, she then adds an explanation. "The building is not designed as a boat. My aim was that it talks about the sea." As we recall: the ship metaphor was one of the most successful metaphors of the International Style in the twentieth century and was frequently utilized by Le Corbusier. But it is today also part of the inheritance of an outdated hardcore modernism in which the architecture of large buildings as machine-like objects stands on its own in a self-centered way—without any reference to a historical, continuously growing urban fabric.

So what does it mean when the architect speaks of the fact that the shape of her big, new administration building "talks about the sea"? It is first with this narrative reference that a link is made to a poetic allusion to the métier of the building owner. In the elegant, blindingly white façade with bands of white marble emphasizing the horizontal, it is not difficult to discover a reference to the global operations of one of the world's largest shipping companies as well. At the same time, the statement also refers to the examination of the contemporary topos of the city in a constant state of flux, which in a way reacts in wave movements to the social and economic upheavals and makes these transformations visible in its outstanding buildings.

1

Kaye Geipel, "Sperrige Moderne, üppige Balkone," *Bauwelt*, no. 29 (Berlin, 2004).

2

Elias Constantopoulos, "Change and Permanence in Greek Modernity. The Case of Takis Zenetos," in *The Challenge of Change: Dealing with the Legacy of the Modern Movement*, ed. D. Van Den Heuvel, M. Mesman, and Bert Lemmens (Delft: Delft University Press, 2008).

Curved Balconies

The new administration building, which is positioned on a trapezoidal plot of land in the second row on Syngrou Avenue, goes back to an internal competition that the client, the Angelicoussis Group, organized in 2012. Sakellaridou's concept, which makes the characteristic spatial form of the urban structure of Athens "flow" in the architecture itself, becomes particularly apparent when one looks at how she has inserted her building structures into the regular street grid of Kallithea. Unlike her six competitors in the competition, the architect conceived her design from the very beginning as a wave, in other words by making use of curved structural forms. The distinctive design idea of working with various layers that structure the building horizontally then arose in the second phase of the competition. The aim of the design can thus be summarized as follows: how can a large administration building with a usable area of 30,000 square meters that is located in the middle of a dense city district also make spatial relationships in the distance visible—in this case as far as the coast of Faliro Bay?

The panorama pictures of the urban landscape of Athens that the photographer Erieta Attali has been taking from different points of view for a long time are here able to provide an additional reference to the design objective. What interested the architect in this case was not so much a literal consideration of the narrow block structure of streets that is part of the essence of European cities, which involves a more abstract continuity in the sense of an urban matrix. The architect was interested in a spatial, architectural statement with which she interpreted the three-dimensional spatiality of Athens: in her building, Sakellaridou takes up the motif of the circumferential balconies and balustrade elements of the typical architecture of residential buildings in Greece. Along with the awnings, these balconies represent not only a climatically important opening of apartments to the open air, they also stand for a "further oscillating" of spatial relationships from street to street, regardless of whether one now perceives them as a pedestrian, whether one looks from one's own apartment over at neighboring buildings, or whether one simply stands with a tripod on a hill in Athens to capture the "city as a whole" as an architectural photographer.

The multitude of different balcony terraces is a distinctive urban design criterion in Athens. Andreas Angelidakis once described this characteristic structural principle of Greek postwar modernism very pithily as the "'balconization' of the Greek City."[3] Since the balconies are simultaneously outdoor living space and assume a hugely important shading function, their functionality also goes far beyond being a pure aesthetic of the city façade, as it shaped, for instance, debates concerning the tectonics of the urban house in a whole range of European cities in the nineties and also found a rather questionable echo in the Berlin architecture dispute at this time.

WHAT KIND OF ARCHITECTURAL FLUIDITY?

"The building opens up to the horizon." In her office on Arnis Street, Sakellaridou shows me various design models that she had built for the decisive second phase of the competition for the Agemar Headquarters. The idea of liberating herself to some extent from the circumstances of the plot of land but simultaneously creating a link to the terrace structure of houses in Athens gradually crystallized: "I finally concentrated on what seemed right to me, elaborating a horizontal structure." With this willful statement, the architect also names the fundamental design challenge of the façade typology with horizontal bands that she utilized. Since, for office buildings, such circumferential terrace areas

3
Andreas Angelidakis, "The 'Balconization' of the Greek City," *domes architecture*, 03/08 COLLECTIVE HOUSING III, http://www.domes-architecture.com/ en/archive/issue_archive_article. php?objectid=903 (accessed August 5, 2019).

are not actually necessary as places for spending time. There are other locations such as the cafeteria for employees to meet.

Office buildings are air-conditioned today, are given glass façades, and generally correspond with the label of an international "corporate architecture." They either reflect a representative postclassicism or are oriented toward the forms of large, globally operating architecture firms and their respective stylistic fashions. Many of the newer administration buildings along Syngrou Avenue adhere to such formal stereotypes.

The French architecture critic Frédéric Edelmann, one of the best experts on a global "corporate architecture" influenced by both American and Chinese urban development, however, recently spoke in a noteworthy essay of a "depersonalized" style without attributes that has come to prevail around the world. Edelmann can also provide a date for this end of "signature architecture." For him, this development is linked to the death of Zaha Hadid in March 2016[4] and to the continuing existence of her firm as an economically successful, globally active factory for architecture.

Designing a Big Building "Like a House"
Sakellaridou did not allow herself to be influenced by such globally familiar stylisms of corporate architecture, but instead translated a design vocabulary typical for Athens into the large scale of an administration building. It takes up almost an entire street block. Only the northwestern part is still occupied by a series of already existing, rather simple Athenian residential buildings.

"My aim was to do a big building like a house, and not like a corporation." In this sense, the architect broke new ground with respect to typology and, with her, the client, which decided on Sakellaridou's competition concept. At the same time, it would be completely wrong to speak of a merely "inflated" house type. Careful translation work was necessary on all levels of the design. For this, a view of the contours of the building structure directly from above, which inscribes it in the plot of land between Doiranis Street and Tagmatarchou Plessa Street, suffices. What can be seen is an L-shaped building structure with a soft line management which occupies the three building corners with an expansive momentum and on Doiranis Street—where the entrance is located—draws back a bit from the edge of the street in a long arc. Along the tapered northeastern side of the plot of land on Lamprou Katsoni Street, this L is supplemented by a circular structure in which primarily spaces for the further training of employees are accommodated. An additional entrance is situated toward this side; the L-shaped structure of the main administration building and the cylindrical structure for further training are linked on the lower level by means of a bridge.

Architectural Elegance
The tour de force that Sakellaridou has achieved with this design shape is an expressive building structure that makes a striking appearance in the urban layout with in part projecting, in part recessed floors and is simultaneously integrated within the urban grid of plots of land. Particularly commendable is the way in which the building structure frames the existing residential buildings on its rear side on two sides, but without upstaging them. The multitiered, horizontal gradation of the bands of the façade also gives the administration building a creative porosity that benefits the various uses. The marble bands at times thus widen to become accessible balcony areas, while they follow the curve of the glass façade very directly at other points. Above all, however, the building embodies an architectural elegance that completely departs from the powerful volumes of large buildings in the vicinity that have been realized in recent years.

4
Frédéric Edelmann, "2015–2016, une Révolution silencieuse," in *Plateforme de la Création Architecturale. Cité de l'Architecture et du Patrimoine* (Paris, 2018).

Megaron Karatza, NBG Bank
New Headquarters, Athens
Architects: Mario Botta,
Rena Sakellaridou, Morpho
Papanikolaou, Maria Pollani
Image: © Pino Musi

5

Pars pro toto, only two publications
are mentioned here: Yannis Aesopos
and Yorgos Simeoforidis, eds.,
The Contemporary (Greek) City
(Athens: Metapolis Press, 2001);
and Richard Woditsch, ed.,
The Public Private House (Zurich:
Park Books, 2018).

6

Evangelia Chatzikonstantinou,
"Fetishizing the Road—Syngrou
Avenue in Athens at the Turn
of the 20th Century" (paper
presented at the 9th International
Conference of the International
Association for the History of
Transport, Traffic and Mobility,
T2M, 2011).

THE CITY AND THE RESPONSIBILITY OF ITS BUILDINGS

The form of the modern Athens of the postwar period, which makes reference at the same time to a unique idea of producing the urban in which many private owners play a decisive role, first came to the attention of international urban research around the turn of the millennium. It comprises a basic urban model that can be reproduced as desired in which the urban house becomes a development principle for a dense but simultaneously flexible city of mixed uses. The tide has meanwhile turned. Since the turn of the millennium, there has been a veritable flood of examinations that also see *polykatoikia* structure as a hitherto ignored, forward-looking model for the European city. Basically, it is about the search for a contemporary development principle for the city which replaces the traditional recipe for success of the nineties, as it was demonstrated above all in Barcelona with its master-plan thinking. While under Oriol Bohigas, Barcelona's head municipal planner, thinking was done quasi from the top down and attractive public spaces were thus integrated into the city, Athens represents a process of development from the bottom up. The *polykatoikia* structure generates a diversity of uses in its ground-floor zones—a mixture that increasingly seems at risk of disappearing from the current neoliberal city—more or less on its own.[5]

One drawback of the Athenian principle, however, is found in the fact that the further development of the urban infrastructure requires its own advocates and competition initiatives—its ability to transform itself otherwise remains limited. This applies in particular to the integration of new urban green spaces but also holds true for the further development of traffic axes dominated by car traffic. Syngrou Avenue is just such an example. Until today, it continues to radiate the archaic quality of a city designed entirely for traffic.[6] Since the nineteenth century this street has been an important route linking the center of Athens with the coast. In the postwar period it was developed into a multi-lane main thoroughfare while dense office, commercial, and residential districts grew up on the right and left. In the meantime the importance of this arterial road has promoted the trend of positioning ever-larger buildings on the sides of it, which, however, also cordon off the neighboring districts spatially. With such office buildings becoming ever bigger, the urgency of considering interesting new typologies for these urban building blocks in the first and second row is currently increasing.

OPEN GROUND FLOOR AND WHITE ATRIUM

The Agemar Headquarters is a formative part of this process of transformation. How does the new building deal with the limitations and possibilities of its location? In the ground floor area, Sakellaridou decided to liquefy restrictive spatial layers. Her building is not positioned on the ground with a massive base. What appear instead are flexible, in part overlapping spatial conclusions that make it possible on the one hand to bring as much light as possible into the basement. On the other, this flexibility allows the building structure to draw back a bit for the representative entrance from the street. Outside here, designed green areas alternate with strongly terraced zones, which makes it possible for even employees working in the basement to go outside directly from their workspaces. The swimming pool and the fitness room are thus also given a surprising green continuation in the outdoor area.

Athens, as statistics show, has a severe lack of nature—the city has only one quarter as much green space as other, comparable metropolises.[7] The open-space planning of the Agemar Headquarters takes this deficit into account. At the entrance and in front of the exhibition space there are two large pools of water, which not only help improve the climate but can be understood as a reference to the function of the company at the same time—the exhibition space incidentally also presents a beautiful historical compilation of the company's fleet of vessels in realistically reproduced models. There are small garden areas carefully laid out around the building, extensive green roofs, and even a vertical garden in the crew area. "Desire arises from little things," the architect notes as an explanation for the fact that every merely conceivable outdoor space has been used for such green interventions.

What impressed me above all is the enormous pine tree, which it was possible to retain despite a complex construction site. Its slender figure rising into the sky today provides a focal point in the newly designed interior courtyard—and simultaneously resembles a compass needle, which contrasts with the horizontal bands of the headquarters as a sculptural counterpart.

Atrium and Routing

One reaches the main entrance via a large flight of steps from Doiranis Street. There, the façade slides over visitors in six bands of white that slightly project ever further outward. Over the entrance, one of these bands also cuts a caper and extends further outward with a special momentum—ready to provide a small protective roof for visitors and to mark the entrance with a small column. On the right and left the vaulting base zone of dark, perforated ashlar focuses the momentum of the façade on the entrance—we walk through the doors between curved walls.

The large central design idea here inside is the circular atrium that extends over all the stories. On the individual floors, it links the two arms of the L with their office spaces as a distributor. This atrium also brings the design motif of the curved bands of the façade into the interior—the flair of Frank Lloyd Wright's Guggenheim Museum can be felt at this central point in the complex. As a hub, this atrium also centers the routing of users; people can orient themselves in the building effortlessly and on their own. But, above all, ever-new and varied views of the garden, the neighboring terraces, and the surrounding city district open up from the corridors.

THE ROLE OF ARCHITECTURE

One of the tasks of architecture criticism is to look again and again at spatial changes in the city specifically where settings of course for the future loom. The part of the city behind Faliro Bay—to the extent that a foreign observer and temporary guest in the city can judge it from a distance—is just such a key location for the development of Athens. For a long time, the urban-planning impulses that were supposed to emerge from the planned turning of the city toward its coast were only set in motion with difficulty. As a person strolling through the city, such experiences can be perceived particularly close up: just a few years ago, it only occurred to a couple of nutty architecture aficionados to walk along Syngrou Avenue. But there have recently been changes in its surroundings. The remaining half of the Fix brewery has meanwhile been rescued as a monument; it now houses the National Museum of Contemporary Art (EMST), which is supposed to open next year following a longer period of preparation. And Renzo Piano's large project, the Stavros Niarchos Foundation Cultural Center (SNFCC), with its ascending, accessible rooftop park, below which the National Opera and the

7
European Environment Agency, "Natura 2000, Spatial Data," in Urban Atlas (2010).

8
Kaye Geipel, "Renzo Pianos großer Garten," *Stadtbauwelt, "Athen und Kassel,"* no. 214 (Berlin, 2017).

National Library of Greece are located, today stands two blocks further to the south of the Agemar Headquarters. Even if one might take a skeptical view of such large interventions in the fabric of the city, which function more based on the tabula rasa principle: the park and the roofed-over terrace facing the sea are a great gain for the city.[8]

The construction of the new Agemar Headquarters is decisive for this city district near the coast in another way. It impressively shows how architecture can exploit its possibilities for dealing with the city, its grid, and its typology under current conditions. The administration building participates with new ideas in the further building of the city and makes an outstanding architectural statement at the same time. Keeping this twofold role of a large urban building for Athens in mind and having formed a convincing synthesis from it is the quality extending far beyond the location that Sakellaridou also gave her building. This building is moreover a model for further buildings in the Faliro Bay Area.

REFLECTED HORIZONS

ERIETA ATTALI

AGEMAR UNDER THE ATTIC LIGHT

Astir Palace Gate, Athens
Architects: Rena Sakellaridou,
Morpho Papanikolaou
Image courtesy: © Erieta Attali

My moving to Athens from Istanbul, at the age of thirteen, was a revelatory visual experience. The foggy light of the Sea of Marmara under which I had spent my childhood was being dispelled by a blinding sunlight, spilling over remnants of the classical world in Attica. This newfound environment contrasted with and complemented the aesthetic I had developed while growing up among the ruins of the Byzantine Romans. In Attica, I found myself surrounded by archaeological ruins gleaming like white teeth, growing out of the ground, eroded but celebrated, indispensable parts of the landscape. And the Aegean, a restless sea, was always in motion under the *meltemia* winds, blasting against barren, rocky islands.

I spent my early years as a photographer documenting archaeological excavations throughout the Ancient Greek world. This provided me with a unique understanding of a reciprocal connection: the relation of the object to its environment. That knowledge eventually became a foundation and bridge facilitating my shift from landscape to architecture photography, capturing environments, natural or urban, in two-to-one-ratio panoramas, always emphasizing the uninterrupted horizontality of the landscape. Since the way I photograph is incompatible with several of the current norms of architectural publishing, the architects that I collaborate with are almost always those who understand the intention behind my view of built space as landscape. It is the same architects who seek this connection between building and landscape in their own work. When they decide to work with me, it is a reciprocal act of trust that affects both sides of the equation architect and photographer and opens up new ways of understanding.

I initiated my collaboration with Rena in the year 2008, photographing the Gate and Canopy at Astir Palace in Athens. Since the beginning, I have looked at Rena's creations as architectural extensions of the gleaming Attic landscape, floating over the horizon, reflecting the Aegean Sea. In 2018, Rena invited me to capture through my lens her new building, Agemar, the headquarters of an internationally renowned maritime group. It was under the strong sunlight when I first came across the white building, which gently curved like an ocean liner, moored between the concrete jungle that is Athens and the restless blue of the Aegean sea, with olive-tinged mountains looming far behind. Rena's Agemar building takes in the fragmented urban chaos of Athens and reshapes it: into white panoramic slices with snaking windows reflecting the sea, and the city itself. The equally white interior whirls up towards the sky, absorbing the concrete tension fully, creating a winding, panoramic continuity that invites the gaze to float and wander.

The horizontality of its exterior and interior is embraced through the large-format camera I use and the two-to-one panoramic ratio. It is multiplied in various frames as a way to look at the reflected horizons, inverting interiors and exteriors. It was a new challenge: the creation of a narrative-based photographic approach where continuity arises through the sequencing of similar photographs. The photographs are frames, but they are also scenes, shifting atmospheres transitioning from inside to outside, always looking through to the city, but also out and above it, into the horizon over the sea.

AGEMAR

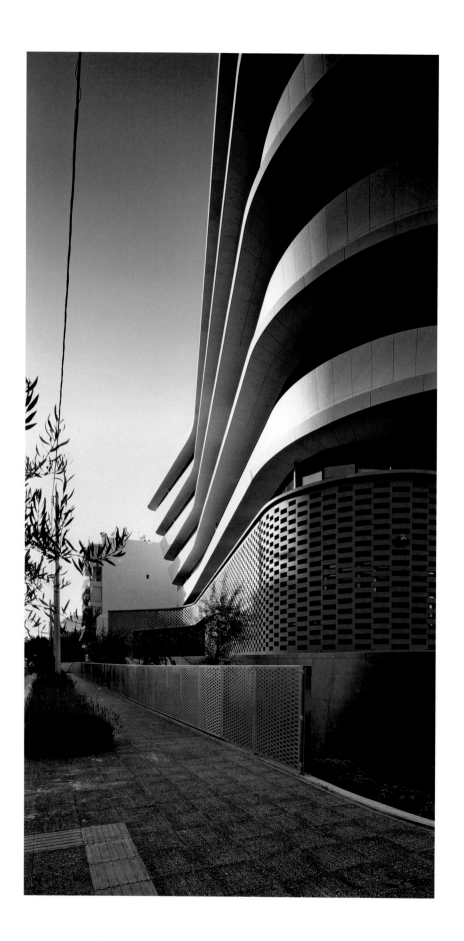

DIARY — THE MAKING OF A BUILDING

RENA SAKELLARIDOU

Image courtesy: © Erieta Attali

ARCHITECTURE IS ABOUT BOUNDARIES

...architecture, I believe, is about space and creating boundaries to define this space. It is a poetics of space and form organized into a whole by means of architectural order, materiality, and light, bringing it all together in a way that I understand composition to be. Our tools are architectural; they are space and form, light and shadow, or materiality, all interwoven into an abstract compositional structure that holds the whole together.

> Is it mere coincidence that all my life I have searched for this whole?
> I search for it in my architecture,
> I try to address this analytically in my theoretical work,
> I try to reconnect all parts in a long journey that goes deeper.

SPATIALITY

...it all starts with the fascinating story of spatiality. The multiplicity of views, the ability to grasp the whole and experience the presence of others by the use of a void, spatial experience generated by geometry or by the fusion of boundaries are tools of spatiality that give architecture its fundamental base.

> Space haunts my dreams, my deeper dreams, the ones I always remember.
> Whenever something really meaningful wants to get to the surface
> of consciousness, I dream of spaces. I again had a dream about a space,
> I say...Reoccurring dreams...
> Space has been important for me since I can remember. My early toys
> were floor plans constructed of little wooden pieces; they were the perfect
> background for my stories of great adventures.
> Later on, when grown up, I would start moving furniture and rearrange
> my space whenever this deep urge emerged to get a new environment...
> I do that to all my buildings. There might be a moment, and most of the
> time this moment arrives and I turn the whole upside down.

DIARIES

I like to keep design diaries. I am interested in the process, not only the finished object. I like to take some distance and follow the ebb and flow of ideas, to listen to the subtle voice that tries to be heard amid the "must-haves" and the "they-want-to-haves." This little voice that brings images, ideas, and concepts interwoven in such a way that one cannot differentiate among them. I follow the ups and downs, frustrations and desires, the never-ending attempts to grasp and to express ideas and notions, hopes and aspirations. I follow the thread that underlies it all. In reality, I follow time in its flow and diversity, for time interferes with the process. What we are is molded in time. One idea gives way to the other in a nonlinear way. An old idea might resurface and offer a new focus to gaze at. We might see what before was vague....

TIME (AND SPACE) WITHIN

There are different kinds of time in architecture. Time for the incubation of the idea. Time for the ripening of the idea. Construction time, "suspended time" as I call it, and the time after completion, time of separation. In every case, time evolves in two parallel courses: one that has to do with how time evolves within us, the other with time that evolves in the external world. It is our internal time, "time within," time of evolution that accelerates or freezes, and it starts again, time that remains suspended between yesterday and tomorrow, dissipated, dispersed and then condensed, time that simply exists, that gives form to the interconnected web of design experience. For ideas gradually emerge…

A STORY TO BE TOLD BY EACH PROJECT

I feel that what we do with our buildings is not just to create environments; we construct stories. We construct narratives made of space and form, of materials and light, of people's movements and experiences; stories of what people do, programs that is; stories made of words and numbers, of intentions, briefs, and budgets, and of relations, a lot of relations, to ourselves, to our teams, to our consultants, to our clients.

These are powerful stories. They may be told in various ways, with photos and drawings, words and numbers. These are the stories behind the scenes, hidden behind the buildings we see. They speak about processes that are never linear. The silent biographies of buildings narrated through the architect's point of view, these are stories that talk about intentions and hopes, obstacles and ways to overcome them, successes and failures. Sometimes the bad guys might win. Or not…

In every project, there is what I call a magic moment that changes what you look at and allows the idea to emerge. This is the moment that, for me, generates the story to be told by the project. This was the moment when, standing on the bridge simulator, I had a sense that a sea voyage is about a destination, that is, a horizon and a direction. But it took some time before I realized that this will be Agemar's concept.

This is the story of Agemar.

Andrea Syngrou Avenue is a major road in Athens linking the city center with the Bay of Faliro; image: Rena Sakellaridou

View on the bridge simulator
Image: Rena Sakellaridou

BEGINNINGS

Competition: First Stage – January 2012

Seven offices are invited to take part in a competition for the headquarters of the biggest Greek maritime group in Athens.

First Visit
I visit the client. I go to the top of their existing building opposite the competition plot. Strong wind. I can see the Acropolis, which is far away. Will I be able to catch this view from the new building? On the other side, the long line of what is to become the linear water pool of the SNFCC cultural center. A strong line, and then the sea, the waterfront of Athens, opens up to the horizon as far as I can see. Boats, the shimmering sea, the hills of Castella and Piraeus, little islands in the middle of Saronic Gulf. The opening of Athens to the sea… I want to find a way to relate the building to the sea, to open it up to the sea horizon.

On the Bridge Simulator
They take me to the bridge simulator. I hold the steering wheel: "I am steering the boat to Antwerp with 9 Beaufort wind." I am thrilled and rather dizzy. "I was born on an island. When I was four, I told my mother I wanted to be a captain," I find myself suddenly confessing to these people I only just met…. Sensing the horizon opening up in front of me, and the direction leading to…I take this picture….Later on, the opening to the horizon, so crucial to a sea voyage, becomes the story to be told by the building.

The Brief Asks for…
The competition brief asks for a "diachronic" building. The client's existing building, on the other side of Doiranis Street, has a marble exterior, in a rather postmodern, neoclassical style. I struggle with the idea of how to express the notion of diachrony. Composition and architectural order can be diachronic, I think. What about mass? Geometricity? The urban scale?

The Urban Aspect
The plot is near the waterfront of Athens, one block from Syngrou Avenue, the main artery that connects the city center and the waterfront. Syngrou Avenue is characterized by large-scale office buildings; one block away though, the area becomes residential. Agemar will occupy only part of an urban block, sharing it with low-income apartment buildings. With a hundred-meter front on Doiranis Street, a low-traffic axis leading to the new cultural center nearby, and with a far larger scale than its neighbors, the urban aspect becomes crucial. How do you compensate for not being on Syngrou Avenue? How do you design a large-scale building within such a varied urban fabric? What do you do when you literally rub shoulders with anonymous and indifferent small-scale housing?

Design Gestures
The curved form "speaks of" the "opening to the sea." We decide to distance the building from the long front of Doiranis Street to relate it better to the urban scale, to create open space and reflecting surfaces of water, to accentuate the vertical dimension in order to emphasize the diachronic. Is this "diachronic" enough? Will we win the competition?

The Bay of Faliro; image: Rena Sakellaridou

Site map of the Agemar building

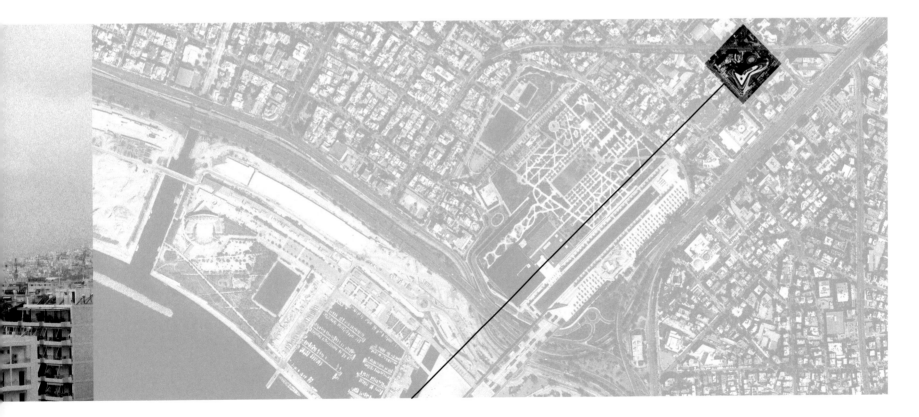

Agemar – connecting the city and the sea; aerial view of the Faliro Bay Area

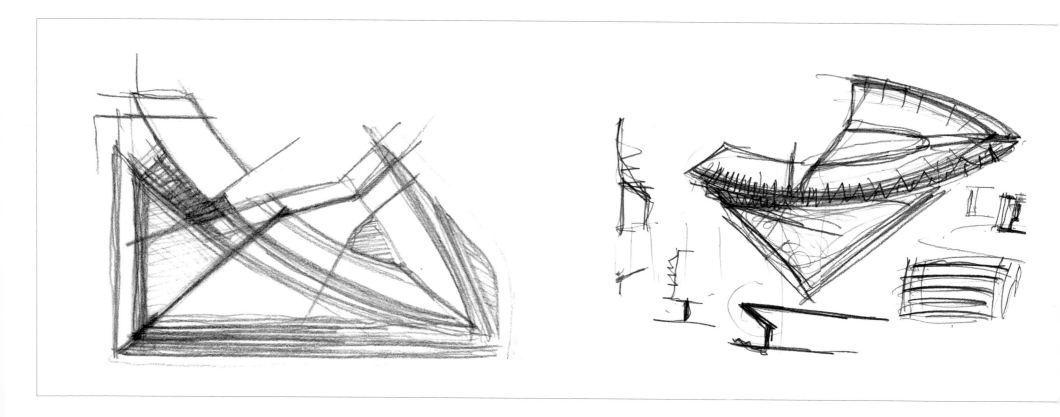

Competition: first stage, sketches and model; image: Rena Sakellaridou

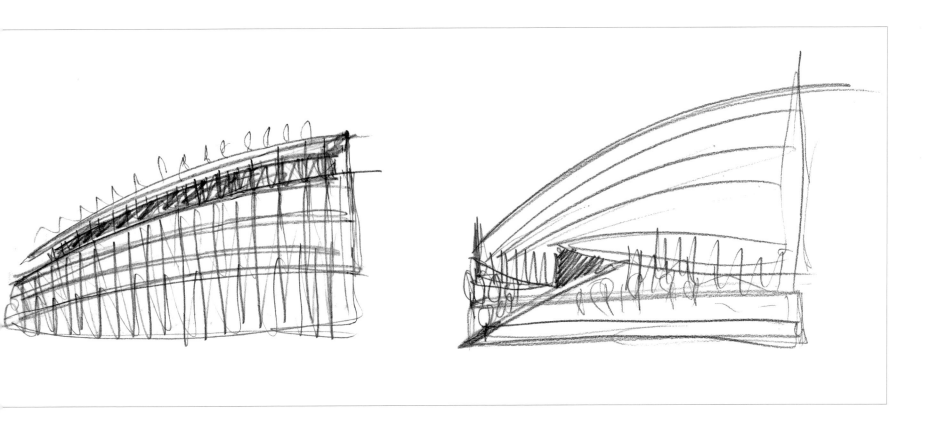

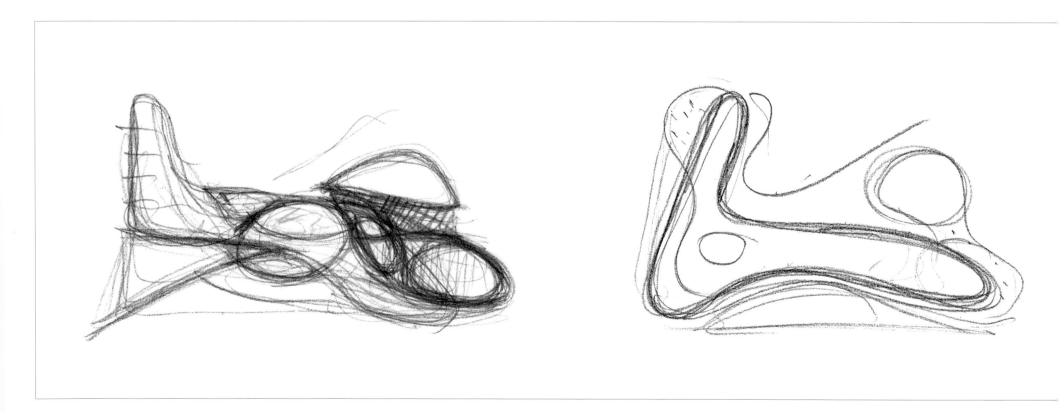

Competition: second stage, sketches and model; image: Rena Sakellaridou

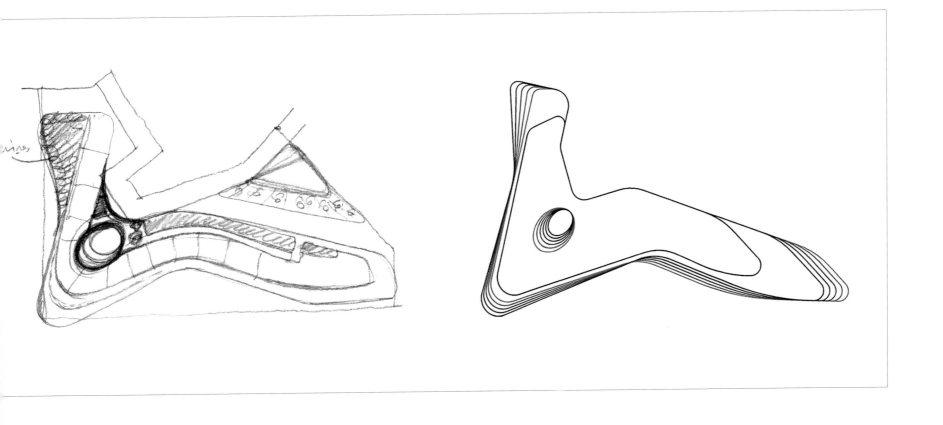

April 13, 2012, 4:00 a.m.
I wake up before dawn with a dream, one of these dreams one remembers for some subterranean reason.... And a realization...

> I woke up with a dream this morning. In my dream, I had decided to dive
> into the deep sea, to struggle with the waves instead of going up to the mountains
> where the sun shines. Swimming into the deep waters means danger, fear.
> Why did I have to choose this? Is there still time to make a different choice?
> I woke up with the feeling that I might struggle with the waves and dive
> to the "sea inside," but will surface again... A liberating thought, as if the whole
> dream is about a sea voyage, as if the boat starts sailing to the open sea...

I realize that the concept I have tried to put into words during these days of the first design ideas is about the destination, about the opening to the sea horizon. Destination gives purpose to a boat at sea. Boat, sea, destination, the opening to the horizon, all come together into what, I realize, will be the concept of Agemar: A Sea Voyage.

May 2012
We submit our proposal.

Competition: Second Stage – September 2012

We are one of the two offices selected for the second stage; we are given a new brief.

> Even though shortlisted, why do I feel disappointment?
> I fear we will not win the competition.
> Having little chance to win, why not be more free in how I design?

The first days of frustration give way to frantic sketching. What was solid and rather rigid in geometry starts to melt into fluid lines. The vertical gives way to the horizontal. Without realizing how and when it happens, the previous scheme becomes transformed into a fluid form that looks as if it is floating on a liquid, the air, or the water. The long front, the entrance at the main intersection, the need to create distance, the desire to open up to the seascape, the movement of the sun become recesses and protrusions, curves of a fluid mass carved in the interior by a vertical void and shaped by a thick façade that transforms the cityscape into a "film strip."
Light becomes a generating element. The open-air public space of our first proposal gives way to a distinct relation of the building to the ground as it rests on a base. Generous carvings bring natural light to underground spaces. Water surfaces generate multiple reflections during day and night.

> In retrospect I realize that, for me, the way the building touches
> the ground is important. It became a conscious decision some time ago
> in a physics laboratory we were designing in Crete; the lasers had to
> rest securely on the ground. At the same time, I was renovating my office
> by literally digging into the ground; I named it "So close to the ground."

Megaron Karatza, NBG Bank
New Headquarters, Athens
Architects: Mario Botta,
Rena Sakellaridou, Morpho
Papanikolaou, Maria Pollani
Image: © Pino Musi

Later on, a house hidden in a garden, the Academy of Athens's new building,
and now Agemar, all rest on a base…
Only afterwards can you start connecting the lines, the way
Megaron Karatza revealed the ancient world hidden beneath its ground
or how the airy curvilinear form of Astir Gate inspired
Agemar's geometry. It takes time to see…

If composition is the art of bringing the whole together, geometry is a powerful tool in this regard. The interior stays simple, organized around an ellipsoidal void that diminishes in size as it moves from the lower to the upper floors and brings natural light through a skylight. Fluidity in program, space, and form is accentuated by perspectives and partial views, continuity in materials, geometries, and transparencies. This is an interior world protected by the deep façade from the "noise" of the immediate environment. From the level of the street to the faraway horizon of the expansive Athenian cityscape, this is a silent world in constant dialogue with the city.

December 2012
We win the competition. Agemar's sea voyage has reached its first harbor.

Image: Rena Sakellaridou

INTENSITIES

May 2013 to February 2016
In a period of almost two and a half years, we complete the design and the interior design. From the initial competition proposal to the construction details, the building undergoes minor changes. The need to find ways to implement our design choices is, however, crucial. Issues regarding the choice of white and gray marble, the substructure and the construction of the curved marble façade, the claustra of the base, the surface of the metal canopy on the roof garden, the vertical garden of Building B, and the curved marble interior walls require numerous sketches, working models and meetings, trial-and-error exercises, and a lot of extensive collaboration between all parts involved.

Having no façade engineer in the team, we rely on our engineers, our consultants, and few contractors willing to experiment with us. Weekly meetings with the client and managers, constant meetings with the entire team, successive working models produced to check spatiality aspects, countless sketches, three-dimensional models, mock-ups, and more than 1,000 drawings account for this intense period.

> Will it be marble? What kind? Which color? How about gray?
> No, it has to be white to reflect the intense Attic light.
> How will we construct the façade? Who will do the inox substructure?
> And the claustra? Will it be concrete? How about GRC?
> Mock-ups, site visits, sometimes almost every day, and some
> sleepless nights…

Design and construction happen in parallel routes. By the time we are in the development-study stage, excavations and construction of retaining walls have started, to be followed by the reinforced-concrete structure. Operating under intense time pressure and facing successive deadlines, timing is an important aspect of the whole process. In the last frantic months, we are all, design team, managers, and contractors, racing against time.

> During the last weeks, focusing more and more on every detail,
> I forget to realize that the building is almost finished. At the
> last Wednesday site meeting, I am told that the users will be moving
> in shortly. Time of separation…

May 2018
Agemar accepts its inhabitants.

Images: Rena Sakellaridou

Images: Rena Sakellaridou

SITE DIARY

I try to capture the fleeting moments of light, space and form,
the ephemeral instances of the building's realization.

"Meteoros chronos" | The Suspended Time of Construction
While during design you get the feeling that time moves parallel to the design process, during construction time cognition becomes reversed. It is then that you might feel time is suspended between what was before and what is to come, but what is to become is delayed more and more....

Like design, construction includes the unexpected, the agony over what will eventually allow the new to surface. Construction, though, perhaps because it so closely involves materiality, gives rise to a special sense of time. You realize, or better, feel the uncertainty of time that becomes divided into smaller and smaller bits and that the actual project under construction is also divided into different pieces of what has to be constructed before and what after. It becomes divided, that is, in a way that brings to mind a kind of "fractal order" in which every bit includes the whole....It seems as if it lasts forever when, for example, even an ill-constructed joint, the absolute minimum, might be seen as a measure of your/their (perceived) failure. And the bad joint becomes so important that it colors the whole with agony and doubt....
For the time it takes for the building to gradually evolve from the virtual to the realized, time remains suspended....

Images: Rena Sakellaridou

INSTEAD OF AN EPILOGUE

A Continuous Whole

At some point, it became clear to me what lies beneath what I try to understand: that people, analogies, geometries, formal rules and proportions, materials, textures and colors, clients, managers, architects, specialties, contractors, technicians, space, architecture, feelings, doubts and agonies, they are all one. They form a continuous whole, a whole from which we, out of weakness or lack of understanding, choose to foreground only parts of and to see only partial views of. These incidents within the continuity of time give meaning to the fragmented succession of designs and thoughts that is our relationship to architecture. It is, then, in these precious moments of clarity that it becomes clear that design and construction, thinking and doing are all one. And time integrates what is set from the time of the concept's incubation to the suspended time of construction to the time that the building is finally finished.

Buildings are hybrids. They are born from the meeting of what already exists and what is just emerging. They are born from the osmosis between what lies within to what exists without. From the internal space, the "space within" that gives each one of us our identity, to its encounter to the external, be it city or landscape, program, people, or architecture, to its encounter, that is, to the whole of the world in its complexity. Our tools are space and form, geometry and materials. Desire, like ideas, emerges slowly. Desire to express this, which ignites the creative spark each time some new challenge appears. Or, the deeper desire to get rid of the unnecessary and to be able to see, and perhaps to do, a little better this time, or every other time.

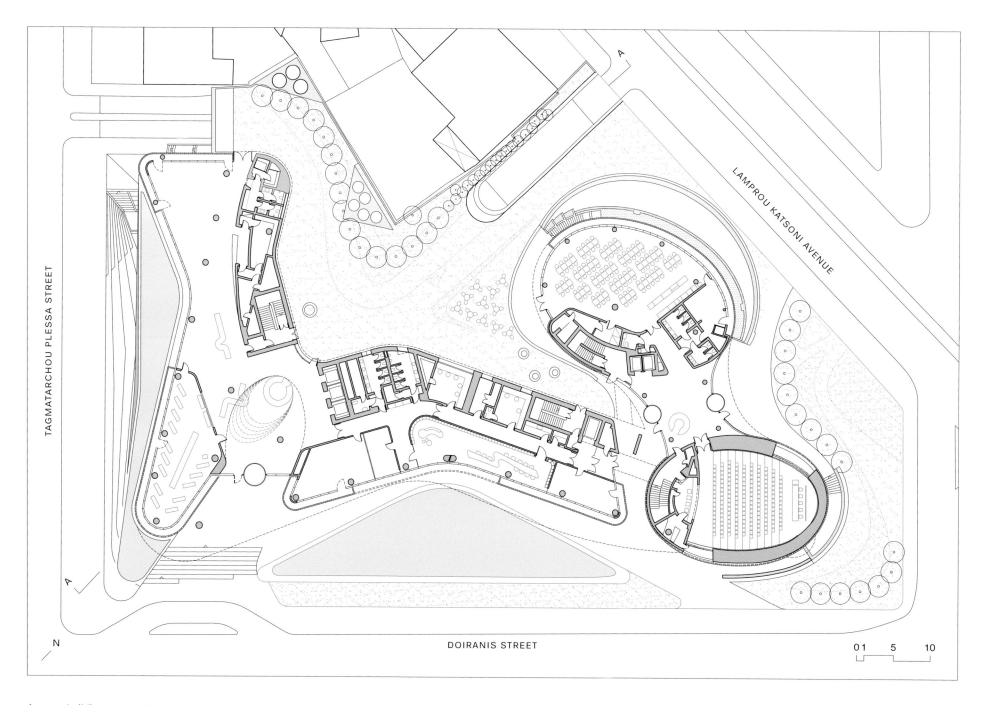

TAGMATARCHOU PLESSA STREET

LAMPROU KATSONI AVENUE

DOIRANIS STREET

A

A

N

0 1   5   10

Agemar building, ground floor

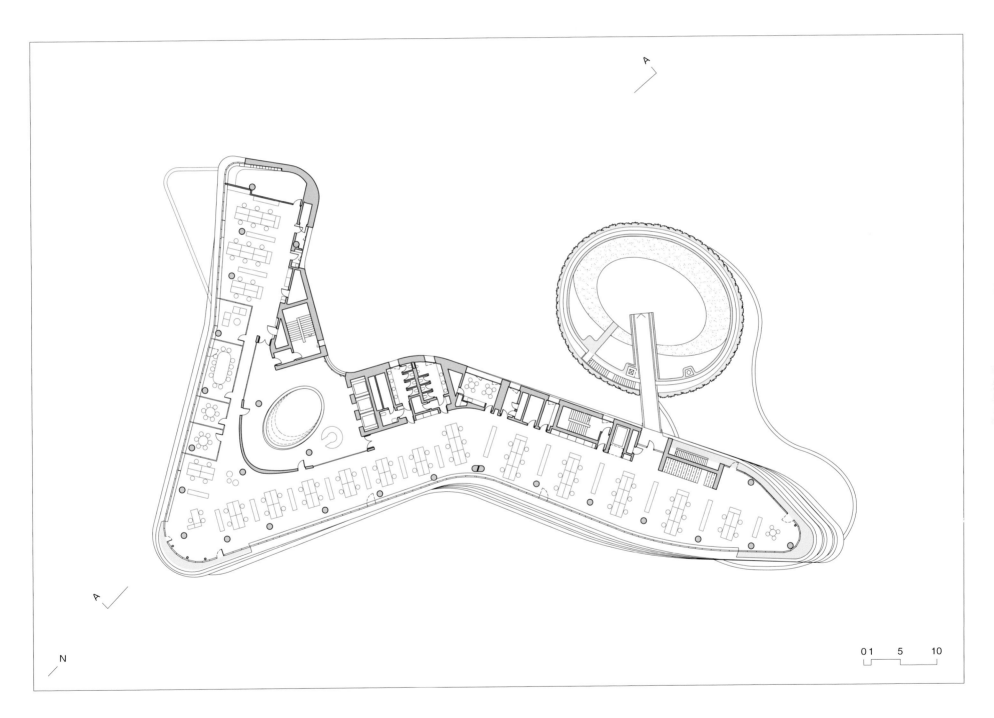

Agemar building, level 4

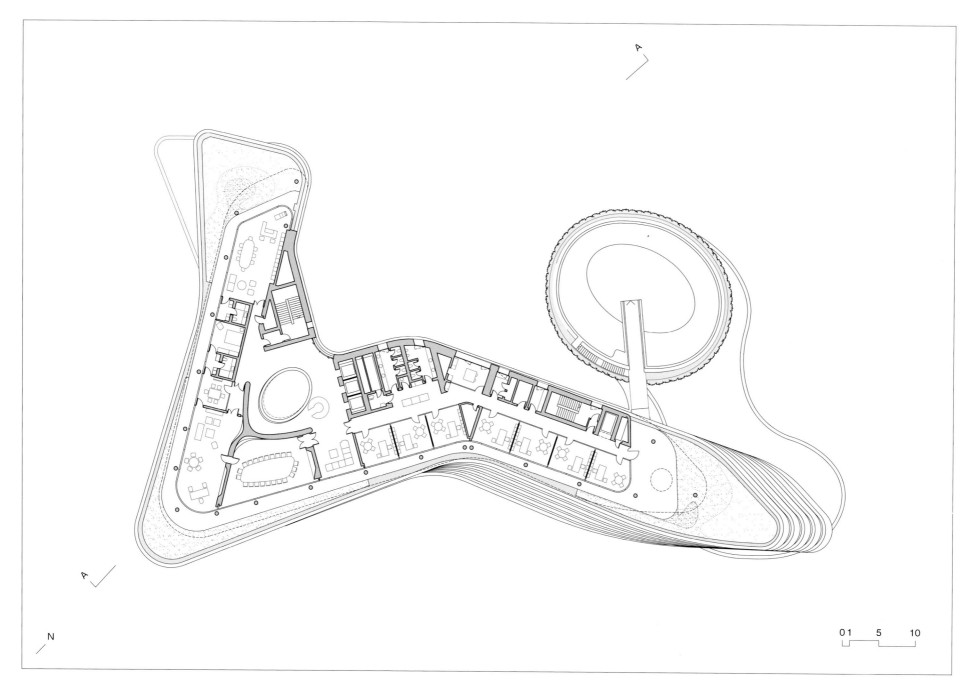

N

0 1   5   10

Agemar building, level 6

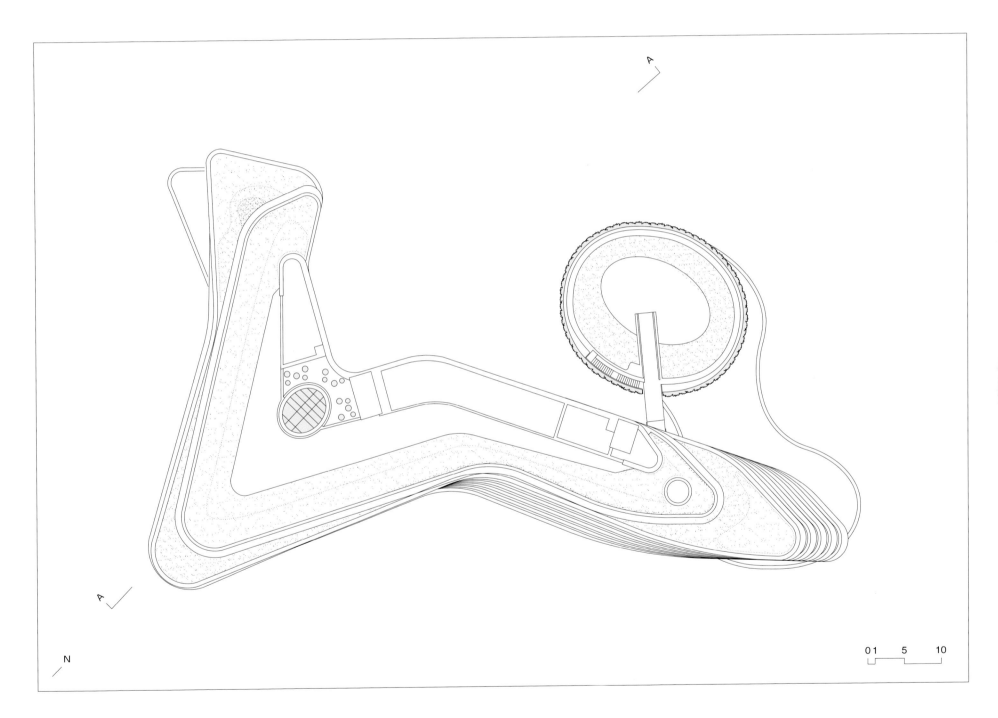

Agemar building, roof

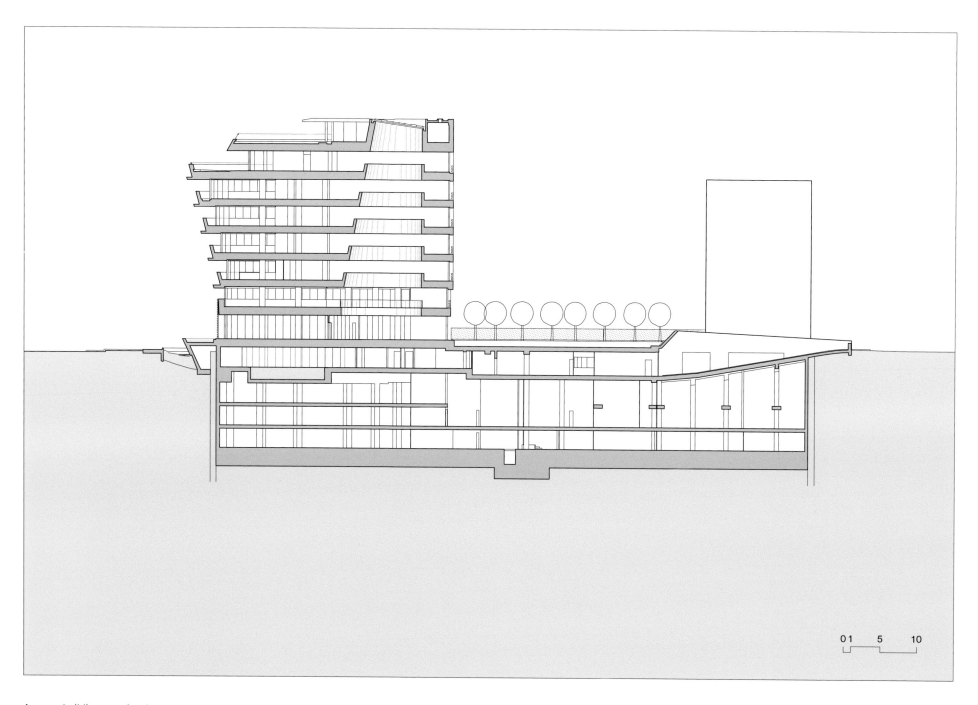

Agemar building, section A

01 5 10

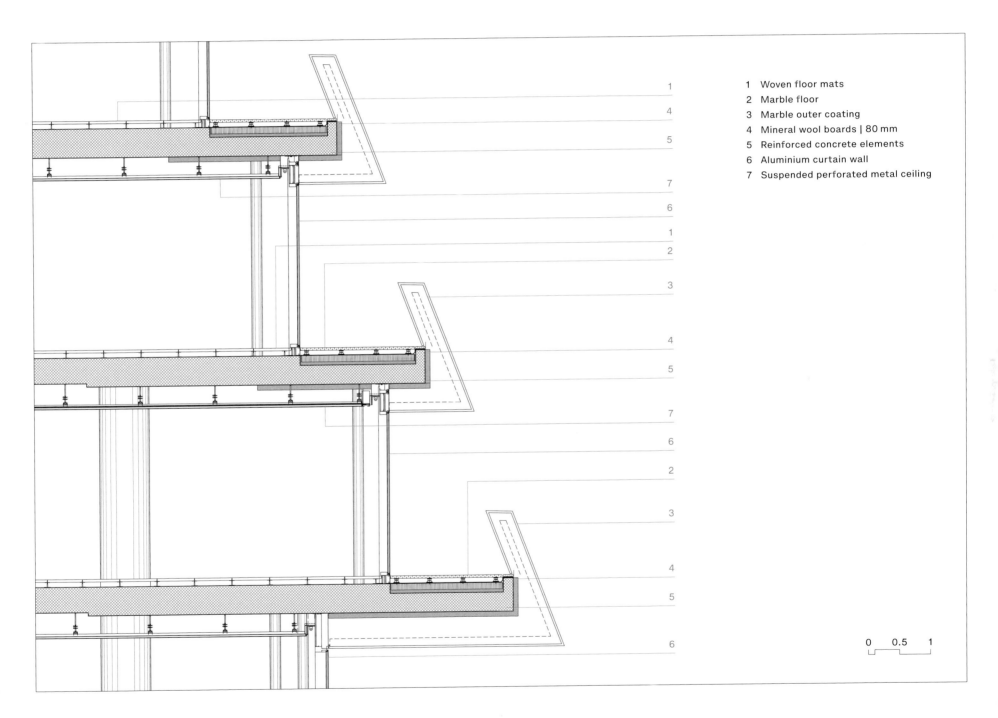

1 Woven floor mats
2 Marble floor
3 Marble outer coating
4 Mineral wool boards | 80 mm
5 Reinforced concrete elements
6 Aluminium curtain wall
7 Suspended perforated metal ceiling

Agemar building, detail

0   0.5   1

RENA SAKELLARIDOU

was born on Samos, an island in the northeastern Aegean Sea, and grew up in Thessaloniki. Immediately after getting her diploma in Architecture from Aristotle University of Thessaloniki, she went for graduate studies to Vancouver, Canada, where she received a master's degree in Architecture from the University of British Columbia, sponsored by a UBC Fellowship. Returning to Greece, she co-founded, with the architect Morpho Papanikolaou, her architectural office in Thessaloniki and later in Athens. A few years later, her theoretical interests led her to London, where she received a PhD from the Bartlett School of Architecture and Planning, UCL, studying the logic of architectural composition. Sakellaridou practices architecture and teaches Design as a Professor of Design at the School of Architecture AUTh. She has written *Mario Botta. Architectural Poetics* (Thames and Hudson, 2001). Design cognition and meaning early on, and recently neurobiology and psychoanalysis, offer her a theoretical base to expand on her design ideas, while always practicing architecture. The very first building, a town hall, extensively written about and acclaimed, led to a number of major buildings such as the Extension of AUTh Library, the National Bank New Headquarters (Megaron Karatza), the National Insurance Headquarters, the Astir Palace Gate and Canopy, the Centre for Plasma Physics and Laser, the Academy of Athens's new building, the House in a Garden, and recently Agemar; to many architectural exhibitions, among them at the Venice Biennale, Milan Triennale, DAM Frankfurt, NAi Rotterdam, RIBA London, as well as in Paris, Montreal, Tokyo, Barcelona, and Moscow; to international and national design awards and distinctions, in WAF, Future Projects Awards, Domes, and the Hellenic Institute of Architecture among them, as well as nominations for the Mies van der Rohe Award and the arcVision Prize for Women in Architecture. Sakellaridou is now based in Athens, and Rena Sakellaridou SPARCH PC (RS SPARCH) is her independent architectural office. She focuses on innovative architectural design in different scales and has a strong interest in the poetics of space, the power of the concept, materiality, and light as the creative forces that allow architectural poetics to emerge into design.

ERIETA ATTALI

was born in Tel Aviv and grew up in Istanbul and Athens. She currently resides between New York and Paris, photographing the work of contemporary architects from around the world. Attali began her photographic career in 1993 as a landscape and archaeology photographer with a specialty in underground burial sites. During the past twenty years, she has been preoccupied primarily with architectural and landscape photography, with a body of work spanning from Europe to the Americas and from Asia to Australia, sponsored by national and academic institutions globally. Her work has been shown in several exhibitions and is the subject of many monographs. The National Gallery of Victoria (NGV) in Melbourne, Australia, has acquired her work for its permanent collection. After receiving her master's in Photography from Goldsmiths, University of London, Attali continued her studies as visiting scholar at the Graduate School of Architecture, Planning and Preservation, Columbia University, New York, with the support of the Fulbright Foundation, and at Waseda University, Tokyo, with the support of the Japan Foundation. She holds a PhD from the School of Architecture and Design, RMIT University, Melbourne. Attali taught Architectural Photography at GSAPP, Columbia University, as an adjunct assistant professor between 2003 and 2018. She has been a visiting professor at the Technical University of Munich's (TUM) Faculty of Architecture; the Catholic University of Chile; the

School of Architecture, Royal Danish Academy of Arts, Copenhagen; the Architectural Association in London; RMIT, Melbourne; the University of Tokyo; Technion, Haifa, Israel; and the University of Sydney, among others. Attali is currently a research fellow at the Académie d'Architecture in Paris and an artist-in-residence at the Cité internationale des arts, conducting a photographic survey on Paris and the Seine. She is the author and editor of numerous books such as *Glass | Wood: Erieta Attali on Kengo Kuma* and *Periphery | An Archaeology of Light*, published by Hatje Cantz, Berlin, among others.

Image: © Jasmin Schuller

KAYE GEIPEL

Architecture critic, architect, and urban planner. Editor of *Bauwelt* magazine since 1995. Since 2010, deputy editor in chief of the magazines *Bauwelt* and *Stadtbauwelt*. Lectures and publications, many of them on the subject of residential housing and city transformation from the fifties to the present. Curator of the international Bauwelt Conferences: "Generation Stadt" on urban density and housing (2014), "Zukunft Energiewende" on climate change in the city (2015), "Produktive Stadt" on a comprehensive understanding of urban mix including city-adapted industries (2016), "Zukunft Wohnhochhaus" debating new concepts of residential high-rise buildings in times of the housing crisis (2017), and "Die Digitale Stadt" on the possibilities of spatial policy to use digitization also for socioequitable urban development (2018). Responsible editor of the corresponding issues of *Stadtbauwelt*. Copublisher of *Public Spheres*, a book about the conflicting changes in public spaces in Europe, using European competition as an example. Coauthor of the expert reports commissioned for the LIN office in Paris/Berlin regarding the International Urban Consultancy Group for the future Development of the Paris Metropolitan Area–"Grand Paris" (2008–14). Visiting professor at the Faculty of Architecture of the University of Cyprus, Nicosia, in spring 2018 on the topic of neoliberal urban development and financing, and its influence on large urban development projects in Europe. Member of many architectural and urban development juries: juror of the "Grand Prix de l'Urbanisme" (2005–2008 and 2018–19), the unique French award for lifetime excellence in urban planning. Member of several European juries: Germany (2005), Spain (2007), France (2009), Austria (2013), the Netherlands (2015), and Norway (2017). Member of the scientific committee Europan since 1999 and board member since 2010. Member of the Schelling Prize Committee, distributing the only international Prize for Architectural Theory in Germany.

AGEMAR
Athens, Greece

Architectural Design: 2013–2016
Construction: 2014–2018

Owner: Agemar S.A.
Owner's Technical Advisor: Melka Ltd
Development Management,
Project Management,
Site Supervision: Dimand S.A.

Architect: Rena Sakellaridou | RS SPARCH PC
Interior and Furniture Design: Rena Sakellaridou | RS SPARCH PC
Team: R. Sakellaridou (architect in charge), G. Chalamandaris,
M. Papanikolaou, N. Apergis, A. Georgiadis, S. Cherouvim,
N. Tsompikou, K. Mastoraki, Ch. Theodoropoulos,
I. Kloni, S. Psirra, A. Doufeksi; G. Papanikolaou, P. Tsogkas,
A. Verteouri, K. Moustakas (model).

Structural Consultant: PCK Pagonis – Polychronopoulos – Kinatos Ltd
MEP Design: JEPA Ltd – Ioannis Papagrigorakis & Associates
Lighting Design: Eleftheria Deko & Associates
Landscape Design: VitaVerde
Parking Design and
Transport Consultant: Dromos Consulting Ltd
Retaining Walls and
Civil Design: OMETE S.A.
Soil Engineering,
Geotechnical Survey: Gaia Ergon – Eleni Kolaiti Associates
Land Surveyor: Michalis Athanasopoulos
LEED Consultant: McBains
Commissioning Authority: VPC – V. Paraskevopoulos Consultants
Environmental Study: Karanasios – Varsami
Health and Safety Consultant: Samaras & Associates
Fire Engineer: Anastasios Pirgiotis
Signage and Wayfinding: Dolichos Meletitiki Ltd

General Contractor: Intrakat S.A.
Excavations and
Retaining Walls Contractor: Geomek S.A.
Marble Works: Smili S.A.

ACKNOWLEDGMENTS

Since my early days as a young architecture student, I have been interested both in design and in understanding how we design. Process and the result of this process alternate in my interests in the years of my studies at UBC and the Bartlett, and, later on, both in my practice and in my academic life. I am a hybrid; I think with space and about space; I design and think about design. Agemar presented me with the perfect opportunity to bring together the two of them.

This book is about a building, Agemar; it would not be possible without it. First of all, I want to express my gratitude to Angelicoussis Group and especially to John Angelicoussis and Maria Angelicoussis for their trust and support through this five-year effort.

A lot of people made this journey possible. Knowing that I might be omitting many of them, I want to especially thank Kostas Panagopoulos, Andreas Terezakis, and Iakovos Zorzos of Agemar S.A., who carefully monitored the project; Manolis Zarakovitis and Konstantinos Kaskarelis of Melka Ltd, technical advisor to the client; Dimitris Andriopoulos, Panos Panagiotidis, Olga Itsiou, Christos Fotiadis, and Leftheris Eleftheriadis of Dimand S.A., who was responsible for project management and site supervision; Petros Souretis, Dimitris Pappas, Dimitris Tamvakis, and their team of Intrakat S.A., the general contractor who monitored construction; and Dimitris Grammatopoulos of Smili S.A., who sculpted the marble façade.

My warm thanks to my team, especially to Gregory Chalamandaris, for always being so knowledgeable, Nikos Apergis, Aris Georgiadis, Stavroula Cherouvim, Niovi Tsompikou, Chrysostomos Theodoropoulos, and Ioanna Kloni, as well as all collaborators who made working together worthwhile.

I want also to thank my consultants: Kostas Polychronopoulos of PCK structural consultants, for expressing architectural ideas in structure; John Papagrigorakis and Tassos Nikolaides of JEPA, electromechanical consultants, and Theodoros Timagenis, acoustics consultant, for their expertise; and Eleftheria Deko, lighting designer, for her sensitive illumination of the building.

A lot of people played a role in making this book a reality: Erieta Attali, with her beautiful photography and valuable insights into the concept; Kaye Geipel, with his exciting thoughts on Athens and its architecture; KOMA AMOK, Stuttgart-based graphic designers, with their graphic design intuitions; Hatje Cantz publishers and especially Claire Cichy and her team, with their continuous attendance to everything big and small.

I should not forget Stavros, Maria, Eleni, and the continuous warm support of Niovi on behalf of my office.

I want to thank Intrakat S.A. for its generous sponsorship of this book.

Lastly, I want to thank Giorgos Triantafyllou, architect and friend, who insisted I make my site diary public.

It has been a great five-year journey; I am grateful to all those who made it possible.

Rena Sakellaridou
Sea Voyage
Photography
Erieta Attali

Made possible through
the generous support of

Editor: Rena Sakellaridou
Photography concept: Erieta Attali

Project management: Claire Cichy, Hatje Cantz
Copyediting: Steve Wilder
Translations: Amy Klement

Graphic design and concept: Joerg Ewald Meißner, Gerd Sebastian Jakob,
KOMA AMOK, Kunstbüro für Gestaltung, Stuttgart, www.komaamok.com

Typeface: Helvetica Now (Charles Nix, Monotype Design Studio and Jan Hendrik Weber)

Production: Thomas Lemaître, Hatje Cantz

Photography processing and technical support: DIGID'A, Davide di Gianni, Fabio Barile, Rome, Italy
Reproductions: Jan Scheffler & Kerstin Wenzel GbR, Berlin
Paper: Condat matt Périgord, 150 g/m²
Printing and binding: DZA Druckerei zu Altenburg GmbH, Altenburg

Published by
Hatje Cantz Verlag GmbH
Mommsenstraße 27
10629 Berlin
www.hatjecantz.de
A Ganske Publishing Group Company

ISBN 978-3-7757-4635-9

Photo credits:
Cover illustration, endpapers, pp. 12/13, 24–27, 92/93.
Image courtesy: © Erieta Attali